Original title:
Trailing Words, Tangled Vines

Copyright © 2025 Creative Arts Management OÜ
All rights reserved.

Author: Olivia Sterling
ISBN HARDBACK: 978-1-80581-863-2
ISBN PAPERBACK: 978-1-80581-390-3
ISBN EBOOK: 978-1-80581-863-2

Echoed Sentiments Among the Vines

Laughter hides in leafy hues,
Whispers flutter, sharing views.
Beneath the twirls of ivy's dance,
Silly secrets find their stance.

Bouncing words on bouncing leaves,
Each joke twists, and none believes.
A squirrel giggles in the fray,
As vines weave tales in a play.

Riddles Written on Petals

Petals blush in colors bright,
They hold riddles in the light.
Bumblebees, with grins so wide,
Buzz around, they cannot hide.

Each flower bursts with tasty puns,
Petal parties, just for fun!
In gardens filled with such delight,
Nature's laughter takes to flight.

Labyrinthine Lines of the Soul

In twists and turns, the jests unwind,
A maze of giggles, well-defined.
Paths of mischief cross and blend,
Every corner hides a friend.

With every step, a chuckle near,
Footsteps echo, loud and clear.
Lost in this funny little game,
You'll laugh, it's never quite the same.

The Poetry of Wild Intersections

Where clovers meet and daisies gaze,
In a tangle that always plays.
A writer's block? A joyful frown!
Just look around; it's all upside down!

The paths we stroll are never straight,
Instead, they cross, they twist, they skate.
With jokes that bloom like wildflowers,
Here's to laughter's endless hours.

Phrases in Tangles

In the garden of chatter, sprouted all sorts,
Whispers of nonsense, weaving wild retorts.
A squirrel did chuckle at sentences spun,
While bees buzzed in rhythm, having so much fun.

Words leapt like rabbits, in a dance quite absurd,
Like roguish little raccoons, they preferred to be heard.
They tangled and knotted, a verbal delight,
As plants giggled softly, hidden out of sight.

The Language of Creeping Flora

Through the thick of the garden, vines crept with glee,
    Whispering gossip like a chattering bee.
A daisy exchanged tales with a proud sunflower,
    As leaves rustled secrets each passing hour.

With petals all fluffed, the stories took wing,
    A lizard looked on, amused at the fling.
They laughed about rabbits, the antics of bugs,
    While roots intertwined like mischievous hugs.

Entwined Stories in the Lush

In the heart of the thicket, stories took root,
A kaleidoscope circus in each leafy shoot.
Frogs croaked out riddles in a symphonic croon,
While branches did jiggle under the light of the moon.

With every green tendril, a tale to unfold,
Of squirrels in hats and snails that were bold.
Laughter erupted, both loud and quite spry,
As the vines waved their arms, saying, 'Oh my!'

Verses Caught in the Thorns

In a tangle of verses, sharp points all around,
A hedgehog recited, and laughter was found.
Prickly and spiky, yet charming in flair,
Each thorn added punchlines without a care.

They stumbled through stanzas that twisted and slipped,
While flowers grinned widely, with humor equipped.
'Not a rose without thorns,' the hedgehog proclaimed,
As laughter erupted and the thorns never blamed.

Whispers Through the Greenery

In a forest where squirrels debate,
Leaves gossip while vines try to mate.
A raccoon in specs reads the news,
While a cactus grins with its prickly views.

The daisies dance to a waltz of the breeze,
While ants serve tea with the greatest of ease.
Frogs croak sonnets to the moon's face,
And the owls, confused, are lost in their place.

Threads of Silence in the Meadow

Butterflies wear stripes, so absurdly neat,
While grasshoppers steal a tap-dancing beat.
The daisies try stand-up, but it's a flop,
As the daisies all giggle, they simply can't stop.

A bumblebee juggles with nectar-filled pots,
While frogs play chess to connect the dots.
A mouse with a mic claims he's the best,
But gets tangled in thistles—what a mess!

The Ink of Nature's Veins

Worms write poetry in soil so deep,
While thorns hold meetings without a peep.
A lily pad hosts a raucous debate,
As snails ponder life while willingly late.

The sunflowers recite with a flourish and pose,
But the poor shy violets just want to doze.
A hedge on the corner gives side-eye so sly,
While a willow just weeps, or more like a sigh.

Inkscape of Life's Labyrinth

In a maze of greenery where laughter is thick,
A worm plays guitar, but thinks it's a stick.
The bushes are jazzed, with beats so divine,
While a hedgehog's karaoke smells slightly like pine.

A frog in a bow tie recites with great flair,
But forgets his own lines—oh, what a scare!
Vines twist like dancers, all tangled in fun,
And the world holds its breath at the day's setting sun.

Vines of Reflection

In a garden, frogs conspire,
Swapping jokes with every choir.
A dandelion wears a crown,
While ants parade in a tiny gown.

Each petal's whisper carries wit,
As bees take turns to throw a fit.
The sun, a judge with golden rays,
Laughs as the flowers sway and play.

Beneath the leaves, a worm recites,
His puns bring giggles, pure delights.
With every twist, a chuckle flows,
In this green realm where humor grows.

A butterfly leaves notes in flight,
While snails move slow yet shine so bright.
The garden's tales, though quite absurd,
Are best enjoyed when all is heard.

Between the Lines of Growth

In the shadows, words do tease,
Whispering secrets with the breeze.
A sprout with dreams of being tall,
Trips on roots and starts to sprawl.

The blossom's giggles fill the air,
Tickling petals without a care.
With tangled twirls, they dance and spin,
A rhythm found beneath the skin.

Beneath the soil, a punster grows,
Cracking jokes as sunshine glows.
Each line of green, a quip entwined,
A playful path that's neatly aligned.

The foliage laughs with every snap,
As squirrels craft a leafy map.
In this chaos, joy is sown,
In every twist of every cone.

Nature's Syllabic Dance

In the woods, the branches meet,
Sharing tales of summer heat.
A squirrel jives with acorn prance,
As twigs and tufts join in the dance.

The brook babbles in cheeky tones,
While rocks roll laughs through ancient bones.
Fungi giggle, dressed in hues,
In their world, there's no bad news.

Fluttering leaves take flight on sound,
Syncopated with the ground.
Each spore a note, each stem a beat,
In nature's song, the laughter's sweet.

A chorus hums through leaf and vine,
While shadows play and twist, align.
In every nook, a jest resides,
In this entangled, funny ride.

Spiraled Sentiments

In a garden where giggles grow,
Twists and turns put on a show.
Words like vines twist and twine,
I promise they'll be just benign.

Laughter echoes, branches sway,
Leaves whisper secrets in play.
Jokes and puns all intertwine,
A funny dance, a twist divine.

Round and round, like a merry-go,
Sentiments flow like rivers, you know.
Each phrase a loop in a daisy chain,
Tickling thoughts, like a gentle rain.

The wordy weeds peek out for fun,
As metaphors bask in the sun.
Spinning tales with laughter's spin,
In this garden, let the fun begin!

Well-Worn Paths of Expression

On well-worn paths, we stroll about,
With quirky phrases that make us shout.
A babbling brook of silly lines,
Tripped on rocks that make me whine.

The road is paved with cheerful jests,
As we explore, it never rests.
Each twist reveals a pun so grand,
Let's slip and slide, you take my hand.

Lost in laughter, we tumble down,
Through wordy woods, we wear our crown.
Bumping into whims and quips,
Let's ride the waves on these laughter ships.

We wander, weaving tales so light,
Turning clumsy turns into pure delight.
With every phrase, we paint the air,
On these old paths, we shed our care!

The Tangle of Inspiration

In a tangle of thoughts, I find a laugh,
Words entwined with a funny graph.
Ideas sprout like tangled trees,
Brimming with jokes and silly teas.

Through leafy twists, my brain confides,
Inspired by chatter and joyful strides.
I dance with puns, I skip with glee,
In every turn, new whimsy to see.

A curious knot that sparks a grin,
Each scribbled line draws a fun spin.
Detached yet close, they intertwine,
In this mess, the punchlines shine.

As humor tumbles, vines create,
A world where giggles resonate.
Untangle thoughts, let laughter bloom,
Inspiration sways, dispelling gloom!

Imagery in the Ivy

In ivy's grasp, I find delight,
Whimsical shapes in fading light.
With giggles echoing in the air,
Imaginative designs weave everywhere.

Twisting leaves form a strange facade,
Imaginary creatures on a promenade.
Each curve reveals a funny sight,
As shadows dance, turning day to night.

Lines of laughter trail and prance,
In this leafy world, we take a chance.
Shape-shifting thoughts take on new hues,
Amusing visions that shake off blues.

As we climb through this leafy maze,
Words bloom bright, bringing laughter ablaze.
In the ivy's embrace, let whimsy strive,
Imagery sparkles, making us thrive!

Hushed Whispers in the Wild

In the thicket, secrets sway,
Bushes giggle, come what may.
Birds gossip in a fancy tone,
Plants blush when they're all alone.

Caterpillars write letters slow,
Tickled leaves, a playful show.
The breeze flirts, swaying each stem,
Nature's jest, a merry gem.

Sentences Twined in Silence

Roots may tangle, words unwind,
A squirrel scribbles, oh so blind!
With acorn caps atop his head,
He jots down all the things he said.

Mice hold meetings by moonlight glow,
In the grass, they tiptoe slow.
Each tiny tale they weave in jest,
Squeaky laughter, nature's quest.

The Rich Tapestry of Nature's Lingo

The flower's fashion, bright and bold,
Bumbles buzz with tales retold.
Butterflies draft their colored plans,
With secret lingo, in flowered pans.

Ladybugs boogie on petals white,
Spinning stories into the night.
Each tiny dot's a verse of fun,
As they dance beneath the sun.

Lyrical Growth

Bamboo shoots rhyme in a line,
Whispering jest, feeling divine.
The grass waves in joyful spree,
While ants break forth in a jubilee.

Clusters of berries roll with cheer,
Hummingbirds laugh, "Come gather near!"
In this orchestra of green delight,
Nature's lyrics take to flight.

Detailed Diction in the Underbrush

In the thicket, words abound,
Fuzzy phrases all around.
Puns are sprouting, growing wide,
Swinging like a jungle ride.

Syllables twist like snakes at play,
With wit that leaps and runs away.
Syntax tangles like old vines,
Crafting giggles with the pines.

Each whisper tickles leaves alight,
Chasing shadows in the night.
A chuckle bounces off the bark,
Where humor hides, a tiny spark.

So join the frolic, do not pout,
In the underbrush, there's fun about!
With silly jokes that leap and fly,
In this wild woods, we laugh and sigh.

Canopies of Expression

Under the canopy, words take flight,
A carnival of sounds, what a sight!
Giggles roam from tree to tree,
Swinging like monkeys, wild and free.

Branches shake with the weight of puns,
As squirrels snicker, oh what fun!
Echoes bounce like playful winds,
In the laughter, the day begins.

Beneath the leaves, a wise old sage,
Tales of folly fill the page.
Jokes hang ripe like fruit on high,
Dodging raindrops that tumble by.

So gather 'round, let your voice ring,
Under this roof, let your heart sing!
In this realm of whimsy and cheer,
Where laughter blooms, never fear!

The Hidden Art in the Garden

In the garden, humor grows,
Petals dance as laughter flows.
A funny tale on every stem,
Where puns and blooms go cheek to hem.

Bees are buzzing sonnets sweet,
Flitting 'round on tiny feet.
With a giggle, seeds take root,
In the soil, joy finds its loot.

Witty whispers between the rows,
Tangled jokes where nobody knows.
The compost heap is full of glee,
A treasure trove of chuckles free.

So wander through this jesting patch,
Where blooms and laughter often hatch.
In a world where silliness reigns,
Find the joy in nature's chains.

Crescendos of the Canopy

Above us, branches sway and grin,
A symphony of chuckles spin.
Leaves join in with playful claps,
As nature weaves its funny laps.

The squirrel's antics steal the show,
Witty leaps, a vibrant flow.
And every rustle holds a joke,
A hidden laugh amidst the oak.

Harmony in every twirl,
As vines embrace and laughter swirls.
A crescendo of whispers fills the air,
With every giggle, troubles wear.

So let your spirit rise and sway,
Join the chorus, come and play!
In the canopy of jest and cheer,
Find the music, hold it near.

Hidden Stanzas in the Wilderness

In the forest, squirrels debate,
Which acorn's the best on their plate.
As branches nod to the wind's tune,
Uneven rhythms under the moon.

A rabbit claims he wrote a great tome,
While dodging a fox, he hastens home.
The shadows whisper secrets and tales,
Of mischief and jokes that dance in the trails.

Threads of Thought Among the Foliage

Dandelion thoughts float high in the air,
While ants hold a meeting, a picnic to share.
The trees wear hats that are twisted and grand,
As giggles erupt from the wildflower band.

A ladybug hosts a debate on the best,
While beetles compose songs that can't take a rest.
With crickets as backup, they sway and they twirl,
In a world where the petals and giggles unfurl.

The Entropy of Meaning

Lost in a tangle of letters and vines,
A cactus tries hard to find hidden signs.
"Does humor grow here?" a snail asks aloud,
As a daisy declares, "I'm not part of a crowd!"

The worms plot a comedy, dirt as their stage,
While fireflies flash like they're setting a gauge.
Each pun is a seed that sprouts from the ground,
As laughter erupts in the chaos around.

Verdant Reverberations

Under the leaves, a parrot recites,
Cracked jokes in a forest, a mix of delights.
"Why did the vine cross the path?" it squawks,
"To tangle with gnomes and stunt their talks!"

With each snap and crackle, the laughter will grow,
As frogs in tuxedos put on a grand show.
Surprise, giggles mingle, the breeze takes its chance,
In a circus of foliage, we sway and we dance.

Reflections Among the Twisted Branches.

In a mirror made of bark, they grin,
Every squirrel thinks it's a win,
Chasing shadows, they spin and twirl,
Cartwheeling through with a whirl.

The branches twist in curious ways,
Tickling the sunbeams, they play,
Oh, look at that raccoon with a hat,
Trying to dance, can you imagine that?

Reflection's laughter echoes loud,
While the bushes boast, they're quite proud,
Underneath, the grass starts to giggle,
As the wind whispers, can you wiggle?

Just a day in the twisted maze,
Where the leaves all share their silly ways,
Nature's jesters, without a care,
Swinging around, with so much flair.

Whispers in the Greenery

In every rustle they tell a joke,
The leaves cackle, the branches poke,
A cheeky butterfly flutters and flaps,
Daring the flowers with gentle traps.

The bushes gossip with playful shrill,
While daisies dance with utmost thrill,
Harmony reigns in a silly spree,
Even the ants march in harmony.

Moss on the ground makes a comfy bed,
While talking ferns nod their leafy head,
They chat about the clouds up high,
And how the moon giggles in the sky.

In this world, laughter grows,
And the laughter blooms, goodness knows,
With every step, there's joy to glean,
In the jolly, jumbled, leafy green.

Labyrinth of Echoes

In a maze where sounds are quite absurd,
Yelling crows share tales unheard,
Echoes bounce, they wiggle and weave,
Secrets hidden, do you believe?

Beneath the branches where whispers play,
Rabbits laugh and frolic away,
Each echo stretches, makes a map,
To get lost is the best kind of trap.

A caterpillar jokes, "I'm almost a bee,"
While daisies snicker, "Not quite, you see,"
Every twist of laughter fills the air,
Life's bright flutters, a humorous affair.

In this maze, we find our tune,
Under sunlight and the gentle moon,
So take a step with a light little dash,
In the labyrinth of echoes, join the splash.

Veins of Verse

Lines that dance with whimsy and cheer,
Words like vines, so lively, so near,
A poet's quip turns into a vine,
Entwined in laughter, oh how divine.

Each line's a twist, a playful tease,
Tickling thoughts like a gentle breeze,
In the garden of rhyme, silliness flows,
With every word, the chuckles grows.

Underneath these intertwining leaves,
Lies a world where nonsense weaves,
Where rhymes frolic, bright and bold,
Like stories from a book of old.

So pluck a line, let it swing free,
In the web of verses, join the spree,
Winding and twisting, such delightful fun,
In these playful veins, we all run.

In the Garden of Expressions

In a patch where puns took root,
The carrots chat, the radishes hoot.
Squash sings softly, cabbage sighs,
As the gossip blooms 'neath sunny skies.

Jokes are buried, weeds sprout tall,
With laughter echoing, a merry call.
Tales of lettuce that once took flight,
Dancing in whispers throughout the night.

Chili peppers share spicy quirks,
While daisies do their happy jerks.
The petunias giggle, the marigolds tease,
In this garden where humor grows with ease.

As I wander through this playful maze,
I trip on puns in a laughing haze.
Nature's jesters, a botanical crew,
In the garden, where laughter is true.

Shadows of Syntax

In the twilight where phrases play,
Syntax dances, leading astray.
A noun trips over an adverb sly,
While commas chase, oh me, oh my!

Puns parade beneath the trees,
The grammar gremlins giggle with ease.
Prepositions jump like frogs in the night,
Creating chaos, oh what a sight!

The verbs are tumbling, such a delight,
With laughter lingering, taking flight.
The adjectives wear their shiniest hue,
In shadows where syntax spins anew.

As the metaphors waltz in a swirl,
The similes giggle and give a twirl.
In this realm of comedic prose,
Words entwine where mischief grows.

Entangled Narratives

Once upon a time in a tangled tale,
Characters giggled, their antics prevail.
Plots like spaghetti, a twist here and there,
The narrators laugh, pulling at hair.

A hero tripped over his own brave feet,
While villains plotted their comical defeat.
Unexpected endings made the readers snort,
And side characters huddled for support.

Fairy tales flipped, and dragons wore hats,
Narrative threads like mischievous cats.
Every chapter a whimsical dance,
As laughter intertwined with every chance.

In realms where absurdity finds its way,
Stories weave in a playful display.
Entangled joys, narratives unwind,
In a laugh-filled world, true mischief we find.

The Poetry of Twisting Roots

Beneath the soil where humor blooms,
Roots twist like dancers in crowded rooms.
With rhymes that spiral in silly grace,
They tickle the ground in a whimsical chase.

The daffodils chuckle with vibrant glee,
While down below, the turnips agree.
"Let's form a band!" they joyfully shout,
Roots wiggling wildly, there's no doubt.

Puns drip like dew on leaves so bright,
While the carrots plot mischief at night.
In this tangled world where laughter grows,
Poetry springs from the roots, who knows?

With every twist, they unravel the sound,
A rooty revue from the underground.
In the rhythm of nature, humor finds rest,
With roots intertwining, life's a jest!

Letters Among the Lattice

Bouncing letters on a breeze,
Dancing giggles with such ease.
Silly sentences take a dive,
Wiggle-wobble, they come alive!

Words in knots like creeping vines,
Jumbling sounds and quirky signs.
A pun appears, I trip and fall,
Laughing loud, I can't keep small!

Pages flip in merry strife,
Writing's more than just a life.
In this garden, chuckles bloom,
Planting joy, we fill the room!

So grab your pen, let laughter flow,
Ink the chaos, let it grow.
In every line a chuckle hides,
Among the lattice, fun abides!

Twisted Linguistic Blooms

Words sprout up in tangled twine,
Jokes and puns are now entwined.
Roses red and violets blue,
Thoughts get tangled, who knew?

Silly phrases start to creep,
In the garden, no time for sleep.
Tricky texts begin to tease,
Whimsical wonders in the breeze!

Giggles grow from every root,
Here's a vine that wants to hoot!
Linguistic blooms stretch far and wide,
Join the laughter, take a ride!

So let's pick words from the patch,
Plant them deep, then watch the match.
Funny blooms, a sight to see,
In this wordy jamboree!

Nature's Prose and Rhymes

Butterflies flutter, thoughts take flight,
Chasing rhythms 'til the night.
In the woods where laughter sings,
Prose is found on feathered wings.

Squirrels chat in a cheery tone,
Jokes exchanged among the stone.
Trees eavesdrop, shaking their leaves,
In this realm, humor weaves!

Boughs that bend and branches sway,
Nature's giggles on display.
A rhyme slips on a mossy floor,
Comedy in every door!

So listen close to nature's play,
Find the humor, seize the day.
In this wild, there's joy in some,
Explore the prose till laughter's done!

Verses in the Underbrush

In the thicket, words collide,
Rhymes run fast and never hide.
Vines entwined with silly sounds,
This forest giggles all around.

A wild whisper starts to tease,
Jesting jokes hang from the trees.
Leaves are laughing, roots may chuckle,
Eager puns in every shuffle!

In the underbrush, thoughts go wild,
Grinning like a playful child.
Witty wonder, mischief blooms,
Verses dancing, fads and flumes!

So join the fun beneath the green,
Where puns are often heard and seen.
In this tangle, life's a joke,
With every twist, more laughter broke!

Secrets in the Thicket's Embrace

In the thicket, whispers roam,
Where squirrels plot to steal a bone.
A raccoon dons a pirate hat,
As birds gossip, 'Did you see that?

Laughter bounces on the breeze,
As bees dance like they're at a sleaze.
A hedgehog claims the crown today,
While frogs croak jokes, in their own way.

The bushes giggle, leaves do sway,
While creatures share their antics play.
A butterfly takes tango flight,
And miles of moss join in delight.

Life's a jigsaw, hasn't a clue,
Each twist and turn brings something new.
So wander on through this wild fest,
And let the nature jesters jest!

The Path of Entwining Thoughts

On tangled trails of thoughts gone wild,
A rabbit hops, his mind beguiled.
He trips on twigs, then blinks and frowns,
As butterflies wear tiny crowns.

A snail debates which way to slide,
While ants march by with claims of pride.
Each thought gets lost—oh what a mess!
Yet laughter echoes, who could guess?

The mushrooms giggle in their piles,
As fireflies light up their smiles.
In every twist of mind's own maze,
The silly thoughts keep thoughts in haze.

So follow whispers down the lane,
With jesters singing, none in vain.
For in the chaos, joy is found,
And life's own riddles spin around.

Nature's Calligraphy

In every leaf, a tale is penned,
By nature's hands, where laughs transcend.
The brook writes verses, bubbling free,
While rocks recite a history.

The trees with arms outstretched so wide,
Share notes of joy with roots as guide.
A crow critiques with caws of glee,
And ants enlist in poetry.

Bramble scribbles in its own script,
A playful notion, deftly whipped.
While daisies giggle, young and spry,
Each petal's joke is worth a try.

So when you read the earth's sweet lines,
Just know the humor intertwines.
In every crack, and every curve,
Is laughter's echo, sharp and verve!

The Interweaving of Syllables

In hedgerows, critters spin their tales,
As laughter drifts along the trails.
A cat sings opera on a fence,
While chickens cluck the same old nonsense.

The wind, a bard with gentle tone,
Plays notes that tease, like a rolling stone.
While flowers giggle at the bees,
And dance along with rustling leaves.

Each syllable a comic tie,
That pulls the fronds in jesting high.
A fox in bowtie shows his grace,
With every step, he sets the pace.

So listen close, as nature speaks,
With twinkling eyes and playful squeaks.
For every word that flits and flies,
Is joy in every laugh that lies!

Secrets in the Thicket

In the bushes, whispers play,
Squirrels giggle, led astray.
A lost sock found by a fox,
Wearing it like a pair of Crocs.

Jokes are tangled, laughter loud,
Among the branches, feeling proud.
A parrot swears like sailor men,
While dancing like it's just a trend.

With every step, a riddle grows,
Tangled tales spun through the throes.
The sun peeks in with a grin,
As trees recite their ancient din.

So come and dance beneath the skies,
Join the secrets where laughter lies.
In the thicket, fun grows wild,
Like giggling starlings, nature's child.

Unraveled Sentences

Words took a trip, got lost in flight,
Commas collided, oh what a sight!
Nouns wore hats, verbs danced around,
While adjectives twirled, shaky but sound.

In the chaos, laughter prevails,
As metaphors set sail on gales.
One lost letter, a game it plays,
Turns 'meat' into a vegetarian craze.

Grammarians sigh, they just can't cope,
As sentences weave like a slippery rope.
A twist here, a turn there, all in good fun,
Try reading it straight, you won't get it done!

But in the mishmash, joy spills out,
Every confused word looks about.
In the snarl, we find what's true,
Unraveled wisdom waiting for you.

The Language of Leaves

Foliage flutters, secrets confide,
Leaves gossip softly, they cannot hide.
Whispers of ferns, tales of the pines,
Catching the breeze in playful designs.

Who knew green could talk so much?
Ducks in the pond, they're out for lunch!
A cabbage shouts, it's a garden affair,
While radishes giggle, without a care.

Rustling around, oh what a spree,
The language of leaves, so wild and free.
"Come join our fun," they hum and sway,
As sunlight dances, lighting the way.

In this green town, laughter abounds,
Where stories of nature spin round and round.
So lend an ear, hear what they say,
In the chatter of leaves, joy finds its way.

Entwined Cadence

Vines twist together in a playful waltz,
Mismatched socks are just the faults.
An unwritten tune hums in the air,
As daisies gossip without a care.

Roots tangle up in a merry dance,
Bees do the boogie, given the chance.
Every flower with a tale so bright,
Swapping their stories into the night.

A giggling breeze skips through the boughs,
Tickling petals, it takes a bow.
Springtime antics, no one's too shy,
As nature's choir sings a lullaby.

Join the rhythm, feel the delight,
In the embrace of the warm moonlight.
With every twist, the laughter grows,
Entwined in cadence, where fun flows.

Lattice of Lost Conversations

In a garden of chatter, they weave and they wind,
With secrets once whispered, now tangled and blind.
A rabbit asked, "Why do we roam?"
The owl just laughed, "It's a giddy poem!"

Beneath the old trellis, a gnome tells a tale,
Of socks that went missing, a very odd trail.
The daisies all giggle, it's quite the affair,
While squirrels take notes with a comical flair.

Each petal a story, each leaf is a jest,
Of garden mishaps, we're never at rest.
They chuckle and snicker, it's laughter they seek,
As vines twist and twirl, oh, what a freak!

So let's raise a glass to the words in the air,
To the tangles and tussles, a whimsical flare.
For in every mishap, in every slight fall,
There's humor in nature, and fun for us all.

Beneath the Boughs of Quietude

Once under the branches, a cat spun a yarn,
About socks that went walking, 'twas quite the alarm.
The leaves all giggled, they rustled in cheer,
As the tale of lost footwear grew ever so near.

A snail joined the party, with stories so grand,
Of journeys with pitfalls, oh, wasn't it planned?
The ferns all shook lightly, in fits of delight,
While the sun sneezed a sparkle, cast beams of bright light.

With whispers of laughter, the boughs gently sway,
As the birds sing their notes, in a whimsical way.
In the hush of the forest, the chuckles abound,
A banquet of giggles, all dancers unbound.

So here's to the whimsy, the laughter we share,
In the shade of the trees, with joy in the air.
For under the quiet, a ruckus can thrive,
Making memories where the silly comes alive.

Rooted Ramblings of the Heart

Amongst the roots, a wise spider spun,
A web of confessions, oh what a fun!
With anecdotes flying, like leaves in the breeze,
They tangled in laughter, brought down to their knees.

A worm chimed in, with a story of glee,
Of a garden party, and who spilled the tea.
The daisies all danced, with petals so proud,
As the giggles erupted, they formed a small crowd.

The toad croaked a sonnet, most curious and sly,
Of wild escapades that flew really high.
While mushrooms took bets on who'd trip on a root,
Oh, the chuckles that bubbled up under the suit!

So let's twine our tales, with roots intertwined,
As nature's own jesters, delightfully blind.
For in every small blunder, in each hearty cheer,
Lies joy in the journey, a laughter sincere.

Cascading Fragments of Time

In the fountain of humor, the ripples collide,
With laughter like water, in currents they glide.
A fish told a joke, as it swam passing by,
Of the bucket of woes, 'twas a ridiculous cry.

Leaves tumbles in laughter, then dance in delight,
As the sun throws confetti, a shimmering light.
With echoes of echoes, they spin and they swirl,
Time's fragments dissolve, a whimsical whirl.

The clock ticked away, but the hands were at play,
As moments turned silly, they galloped in sway.
With each second twisting into a new rhyme,
The world turned to laughter, in cascading time.

So raise up your voices, let the humor ignite,
In the dance of the hours, all shadows take flight.
For every tick-tock brings chuckles divine,
Like water through stones, may we always entwine.

Organic Syntax

In the garden of my mind, plants confuse,
Sentences sprout with a curious fuse.
Nouns twist and turn like a game of charades,
Verbs take a leap, in their playful parades.

Adjectives dance like leaves in the breeze,
Punctuations giggle like bees in the trees.
Each line a vine that leads to a joke,
Weaving wordplay with laughter, a lark for the folk.

With roots in the soil, ideas become,
A jigsaw of phrases, all tangled and fun.
Awkwardly blooming in the sun's warm embrace,
Language is messy, but we smile at its face.

So let's harvest laughter from this leafy ground,
With each quirky phrase, a new giggle is found.
An orchard of puns where confusion will twine,
In this funny garden, our thoughts intertwine.

Enigma of the Vines

A grapevine whispers secrets so sly,
With words that wiggle and often deny.
They intertwine humor, like socks in a wash,
And sneak through my thoughts in a whimsical posh.

Each twist of the vine tells a tale of delight,
Of rhymes that take flight on a giggle-filled night.
Ask a fruit what it means to be ripe,
And it'll answer back with a playful new type.

The leaves are conspiring, they don't want to fall,
They cling to their humor, bursting out in a sprawl.
Beneath the rich soil, nonsense takes root,
Producing puns daily, like fruits in pursuit.

So come, dear friends, let's unravel this jest,
In the enigma of vines, we'll find our best quest.
With laughter as our guide, we'll dance through the maze,

Finding joy and confusion in wordy displays.

Words Growing Wild

In a patch of strange phrases, words sprout and thrive,
With humor and chuckles helping them jive.
Each syllable dances, a cartoon on screen,
As thoughts grow in tangles, unseen and obscene.

A pun in the corner is hoping for light,
While grammar's wild party goes on through the night.
Nouns wear odd hats and verbs play charades,
Adjectives tumble, ignoring barricades.

Let's sip on the nonsense, like tea in a cup,
With laughter as sweet as a hiccuping pup.
We'll gather the giggles, like apples in crates,
And craft a fine orchard of marvelous states.

So join me in folly, where words bloom and cheer,
In this wild garden where laughter is near.
With whimsy as our compass, we'll venture and roam,
In this jungle of letters, we'll find our sweet home.

Threads of Imagination

In the loom of my thoughts, threads twist and entwine,
Weaving stories where nonsense is fine.
Each fiber a whimsy, a jolly delight,
Crafting smiles that shimmer, oh what a sight!

Patterns emerge when words run amok,
With puns and jokes that are lightly unlock.
Don't mind the tangle, embrace the unique,
For laughter's the endgame, that's all we seek.

A tapestry bright, with colors galore,
Creating a quilt where imaginations soar.
Each stitch is a giggle, each knot is a tease,
In this fabric of fantasy, we do as we please.

So let's spin our tales, let the chaos commence,
With threads of our thoughts, we'll play with suspense.
In this boundless design, where fun never ends,
We'll revel together, for joy is our friend.

Embraced by Nature's Prose

In a meadow, I found a sock,
Hiding under the old oak rock.
The wind whispered secrets, oh so sly,
While bees played tag, buzzing by.

A squirrel wore a tiny hat,
Scampering sideways, what a chat!
Flowers giggled, their petals swayed,
As nature's joke parade displayed.

A worm wiggled with utmost pride,
Screaming, "I'm earth's best glide!"
While daisies danced a silly jig,
Underneath a sleeping pig.

The sun winked, with a golden grin,
Saying, "Join me, let the fun begin!"
Laughter echoed through the trees,
Life's a punchline, if you please!

The Serenade of Climbing Shadows

A vine stretched high to touch the skies,
With leafy fingers, it tried to rise.
But tripped on a branch, what a sight,
Falling down in pure delight.

A turtle sang a serenade,
While lizards formed a grand parade.
Crickets played an offbeat tune,
As fireflies flickered, bright as noon.

The shadows danced with utmost glee,
Throwing shapes that no one could see.
A raccoon joined, with a twisty prance,
And the night giggled at their dance.

Stars chuckled down, their twinkles bright,
Joining in on the silly night.
In the crook of an ancient tree,
Nature's hilarity was the key!

Portraits of the Twisting Path

A crooked path through brambles led,
To a place where words often fled.
Each step I took, a laugh I heard,
From a misplaced, chirpy little bird.

With every twist, the trail would bend,
Revealing secrets around each end.
A gnome peeked out, with a toothy grin,
Saying, "I'm the path's greatest win!"

Trees shrugged off their leafy coats,
While ants composed their tiny notes.
Raccoons strummed on fallen wood,
Making music as only they could.

At the end of the trail's embrace,
I found my place, a funny space.
Where roots whispered tales of fun,
And I joined in, a jester on the run!

The Language of Flourishing Foliage

In a garden filled with shades of green,
Whispers of laughter could be seen.
Petunias wore a fancy gown,
As roses shared their thorny frown.

The daisies chattered, sharing news,
While lilacs danced in polka shoes.
A bumblebee with a Bobby pin,
Buzzed his way to join the din.

Leaves shook hands, like old pals do,
Trading quips 'bout morning dew.
A sunflower winked with all its might,
Claiming, "I'm tallest, just for spite!"

The branches swung, a merry crew,
Creating mayhem with each hue.
In this place where laughter thrives,
Nature speaks, and humor lives!

The Mystery of Verdant Expressions

In the garden of chatter, with quirks and laughs,
A squirrel named Chuck plots poetic paths.
He trips on his tongue, with a snicker and jest,
While vines twist around, putting puns to the test.

A flower in yellow, it giggles a rhyme,
Mixing up metaphors, oh what a crime!
The cactus gives side-eye to all the commotion,
As grasshoppers tap dance, causing a notion.

With every green leaf, a secret reveals,
A joke buried deep, behind bushy appeals.
Sticky fingers of ivy, they tickle and tease,
Making words wobble, like wobbly cheese.

So come take a stroll, where the laughter entwines,
In the wild mysteries of verdant designs.
A riddle that's leafy, with petals aglow,
In the funny bouquet where the giggles do grow.

Verse in the Twisted Palisade

In a forest of phrases, where shadows twirl,
Nonsense hangs low like a zany pearl.
With branches that giggle, and trunks that are sly,
Words wander about, like a confused butterfly.

A rabbit in glasses, reciting a script,
While owls shake with laughter, their wisdom eclipsed.
The trees mumble whispers with tongues full of glee,
As roots tie together like friends at a spree.

Moss cushions the ground, like a giggling bed,
Where verses erupt from the chaos ahead.
In this palisade's heart, the quirkiness thrives,
Fables tickle the air, keeping humor alive.

So roam through this maze of jumbled delight,
Where each crooked corner invites you to write.
A map made of laughter, with riddles to spare,
In the verse of the twisted, all mischief laid bare.

Grappling with Grammar

A comma stumbles across a full stop's plea,
While nouns play a game of hide and seek glee.
Verbs do the cha-cha and then spin around,
While adjectives giggle, their colors abound.

Prepositions are tangled like shoelaces lost,
Adverbs skip by, like they're dancing, embossed.
The subject now puzzled, must choose which to bring,
While pronouns just giggle, not caring a thing.

In this grammar gym, we flex our minds wide,
As syntax twists playfully, taking us for a ride.
With mischief in language, we frolic and play,
Riddles in letters, our own cabaret.

So grab your punctuation, and let's have a ball,
In a world where words trip, yet we love them all.
Join the circus of grammar, where silly shines bright,
In this fun-tangled dance of the letters' delight.

Metaphors Like Wildflowers

In a field of odd phrases, where flowers bloom wide,
Metaphors giggle, with colors that glide.
The daisies are playful, the daisies are keen,
Each one a riddle, in tints of bright green.

Butterflies flutter with whispers of cheer,
As similes tiptoe, bringing smiles near.
With laughter like petals, they swirl in the breeze,
Making every cold turn feel as warm as a tease.

A tulip in pink, throws a pun so divine,
While dandelions chuckle, inviting us to dine.
In this garden of wordplay, the mirth's never done,
As lovely comparisons dance in the sun.

So wander this wildflower patch filled with glee,
Where laughter's the nectar, as sweet as can be.
With metaphors blooming, in quirky designs,
We're left with the magic of fanciful lines.

In the Garden of Unsaid Things

In a garden of thoughts left unspun,
Whispers dance as they come undone.
Laughter grows where ideas might flop,
Plants of mischief, they sprout and hop.

A flower with secrets, wearing a grin,
Could tell you tales, but where to begin?
Bumblebees giggle at the things they hear,
Buzzing in harmony, spreading good cheer.

The sun has a joke that it shines on the blooms,
While shadows chuckle in their cozy rooms.
Gnomes play poker, betting with smiles,
As butterflies flutter, adding to their styles.

In this wild patch, hilarity springs,
Where nothing is clear, but joy simply clings.
Petals are poets, writing in haste,
Crafting their verses with a whimsical taste.

Excerpts from the Woodland Diary

Dear log, today I overheard a crow,
Telling wise tales that make no sense, though.
Acorns clacked in a debate with the breeze,
While rabbits attempted their best stand-up tease.

I wrote of a squirrel who dreamed he could fly,
With wings made of twigs and a very big pie.
Owls rolled their eyes, oh, what a sight!
As frogs croaked along with all of their might.

Mice held a concert on top of a rock,
While beetles performed their best trick with a clock.
The pines giggled softly, their needles aflutter,
As dawn brought a breeze with a hint of warm butter.

I'll pen a new chapter about dancing ferns,
And mushrooms that boast of their scholarly turns.
Every creature is part of this woodland spree,
Where nonsense and laughter are wild and free.

The Tangle of Dreams and Delusions

In a maze of thoughts where confusion takes flight,
A dreamer can stumble, but that's all right!
Cacti argue with clouds about rain,
While shadows stand guard and plead to explain.

A ladybug claims she's a queen of the air,
With a crown made of grass and a wildflower flair.
Toads tell tall tales of their time at the ball,
As crickets compose a grand symphonic call.

Hopscotch is played on the edges of dreams,
With ribbons of laughter flowing in streams.
The moon puts on skits, a glowing charade,
While mice start a riot, a curfew delayed.

In this delightful mess, the norm gets unspooled,
And sanity's surely been thoroughly fooled.
Embrace all the quirks, let the chaos unfurl,
As we swirl in delight, in this whimsical whirl.

A Mosaic of Liaisons in Bloom

In the garden of antics, what a grand scene,
Lovelorn plants whisper, their feelings are keen.
Every flower is dating, oh what a sight!
As thorns shake their heads, not ready to bite.

The daisies are giggling with dandelions, too,
While roses compose sonnets all shiny and blue.
Bees throw a party, with petals as hats,
And butterflies flutter in digital chats.

Caterpillars boast of their fashion and flair,
While mushrooms shake hands with the chilly night air.
Love notes are written on leaves with finesse,
Oh, the drama unfolds—a botanical mess!

Each branch is a gossip, each stem is a friend,
In this quirky romance, the laughter won't end.
We twirl with the joy that blossoms in spring,
As nature unravels the wildest of things.

Burgeoning Ballads

In gardens wild, tales twist and spin,
The daisies gossip while weeds sneak in.
A dandelion sways with airs so bold,
Claiming it's royalty, a sight to behold.

The ants hold cauldrons, brewing up glee,
While squirrels craft poems above by the tree.
They write on leaves, with acornish pens,
Of the grand adventures of long-lost friends.

Intertwined Imaginations

In tangled brushes, daydreams abound,
Where fairies dance wildly, lost and found.
A cat in a hat recounts his great chase,
While shadows play tag, joining the race.

The vines weave stories, laughter and cheer,
Chasing the sunbeams, guiding us near.
A curious snail drags its house on the ground,
Murmuring secrets of life all around.

The Understory of Connection

Beneath the tall trees, vines twist and twine,
Creating sweet stories in their own design.
A beetle next door shares hilarious tales,
Of how he outsmarted the wind and the gales.

A mushroom throws parties, mushrooms galore,
While fireflies giggle, glowing like lore.
The breeze joins in, tickling all the leaves,
Crafting a symphony the forest believes.

Nature's Echo Chamber

In the echo of leaves, a raccoon sings loud,
A parody tune, all the critters are proud.
A tree stump recites in a voice so grand,
Of woodland escapades, oh how they planned!

The brambles make jesters, bows on their heads,
Drawing up laughter from the whimsical spreads.
While croaking frogs croon, in sync with the breeze,
Telling tales of mishaps under the trees.

Vines of Memory entwined

In a garden of thoughts, I trip and fall,
With ankle-length dreams that fumble and sprawl.
Grapevines of laughter twirl 'round my mind,
As memories dance, a wobbly bind.

Whimsical whispers weave through the air,
Reminding me of moments, strange and rare.
A squirrel once juggled acorns with glee,
But slipped on a leaf, oh, how fun it could be!

Each thought is a flower, each giggle a sprout,
Entangled in nonsense, there's no easy route.
With every mishap, I can't help but grin,
These wild, winding tales invite me to spin.

So here I stand, tangled in my own tale,
In a vine-twisted world, I merrily sail.
Laughter's the sunlight, the roots run so deep,
In this maze of mirth, I'm ready to leap.

Chronicles Among the Leaves

Once in a forest of thoughts so spry,
I met a wise owl who taught me to fly.
He hooted with joy, then tripped on a twig,
His wisdom was grand, but he danced like a pig.

The leaves shared their gossip, all rustles and flaps,
Of squirrels in suits, and raccoons with maps.
Each branch held a story, bright as a sunshine,
While clouds rolled their eyes at this merry design.

A chipmunk debated the price of a nut,
While a snail took the stage in a dramatic strut.
Oh, what a jumble of antics occurred,
The trees shook with laughter, each verse sweetly blurred.

In this leafy domain, where silliness grows,
I scribble my tales as the laughter bestows.
For in every whisper, a giggle is found,
In my chronicles here, joy is unbound.

Synaptic Twists in the Wild

In a jungle of thoughts, neurons collide,
With ideas that tumble, and giggles that ride.
A monkey flips memories in playful delight,
While the parrot squawks wisdom, albeit a fright.

Thoughts coil like vines, each one wrapped in jest,
As critters concoct their own wild fest.
A hedgehog on roller skates zooms past my ear,
Spouting profound nonsense that's nothing but clear.

Between chuckles and chuckles, the giggles grow loud,
As the wild things keep pondering, "What's in a cloud?"
A raccoon in pajamas steals marshmallows, too,
In this place of absurdity, fun is the glue.

So I wander through synapses and whimsical beams,
Searching for laughter hidden in dreams.
With each twist and turn, I find joy unconfined,
In this land of strange thoughts, where humor's aligned.

Echoes Beneath the Underbrush

In the thicket below, where the giggles reside,
I found a lost sock, who claimed it could glide.
A rabbit in slippers was trying to dance,
With a hat made of lettuce—what a curious chance!

The whispers of bushes shared tales of the past,
Of squirrels in love, running fast, oh so fast.
The echoes of laughter bounced off every tree,
In a chorus of nonsense that tickled me free.

Among roots and the brambles, the stories unwind,
Of gophers who juggle, and hedgehogs entwined.
Each bush held a secret, each vine had a jest,
While frogs croaked out songs—a wild, funny fest!

So here in this underbrush, I frolic and play,
With echoes of laughter that brighten my day.
In this tangled-up world, the chuckles prevail,
As joy rides the currents of each leafy trail.

Lush Lexicons

In the garden where puns grow tall,
A joke sprouted, could it be a prank call?
Words twist and turn, on a merry spree,
Dancing like squirrels, so wild and free.

Merriment hidden in each leaf's fold,
Witty whispers from the brave and bold.
A quip like a whirlwind, round and round,
Making the dullest moments resound.

With every chuckle, the blooms become bright,
Laughter erupts, what a glorious sight!
Like playful kittens chasing their tails,
In this wordy wonderland, joy never fails.

So gather your phrases, let them take flight,
In this lush lexicon, all feels just right!
Create a bouquet from the silly and sweet,
In the garden of giggles, life's ever neat.

The Forest of Figurative Speech

In a forest where metaphors play hide and seek,
Trees tickle the clouds with their cheeky peak.
Similes swing from branches so high,
Cackling squirrels burst forth with a sigh.

Underfoot lie puns that wiggle and weave,
Entangled with roots, who can believe?
Each step a jest, with giggles around,
The trunks whisper secrets, a riddle profound.

In the shadows, irony loves to roam,
Making sports of the wooden gnome.
A pinecone offers a riddle or two,
Sparking joy with each word it drew.

By dawn's early light, laughter's the sounds,
In this lively forest, pure joy abounds.
Impossible to fret when the sun shines bright,
In the realm of the quirky, everything's right.

Unbound Thoughts

Riddles frolic like butterflies free,
Ideas flutter, oh what glee!
A tangle of thoughts, amusing and bright,
Creating a storm in the middle of night.

Jokes unspool like yarn from a kitten,
Chasing their tails, laughter is written.
Witty as shadows, they leap and dive,
Making the mundane feel so alive.

In a web of whimsy, creativity twirls,
A cacophony of giggles, like dancing swirls.
Each twist a chuckle, each turn a grin,
In unbound moments, pure joy begins.

Catch the jest in the winds of change,
Here in this realm, nothing feels strange.
So come, let's ponder this playful maze,
With a heart full of laughter, we'll set it ablaze.

Nature's Poetic Embrace

In the arms of nature, jokes grow so bright,
Tickling the earth under moon's soft light.
Branches sway gently, a playful tease,
As whispers of humor dance in the breeze.

Clouds float by with a wink and a laugh,
Sunshine spills joy, like a friendly giraffe.
Each petal a pun, every leaf a jest,
Nature's comedy club, oh, it's the best!

A brooks bubbling laughter, soft and sweet,
Echoing the giggles of springtime greet.
In this vibrant world, no space for gloom,
Jokes blossom brightly, in full bloom.

So here's to the quirk in the greenery,
Where every chuckle is pure scenery.
Join the merriment, let nature ignite,
In this playful embrace, everything's right.

Enchanted Enclosures

In a garden filled with chatter,
A snail wore a hat like a gaffer.
The daisies danced, they said,
"Look out for the gopher's clever swagger!"

Bouncing bees said, "What a sight!"
As they sipped nectar, feeling alright.
A worm wiggled in a sock,
While the grass made its grand delight!

A hedgehog laughed, spun in a twirl,
While a butterfly fluffed its swirl.
Each plant had a story to share,
In this quirky, leafy whirl!

The sun threw a party, bright and bold,
With the trees wearing hats of gold.
Laughter echoed, petals unfurled,
In this garden of joy uncontrolled!

The Frolic of Foliage

In the brush where the squirrels gleam,
A raccoon plotted its snack-time scheme.
Knocking over acorns with glee,
"I'm the snack king!" it would scream.

The ferns twirled, in a merry dance,
Spreading tales of a caterpillar's prance.
"Who tied my leaves in knots today?"
Cracked the woodpecker with a glance.

Branches wielding a vine's embrace,
Tangled vines turned into a race.
Laughter arose as they spun and twined,
In this whimsical garden space!

The blossoms giggled, swayed with cheer,
As they welcomed the butterflies near.
With each bloom flaunting a colorful whim,
Nature's oddball concert was here!

Whimsy Among the Willows

Under the willows, kittens played,
Chasing shadows that danced on parade.
They giggled at birds who forgot their tunes,
As laughter settled, no need for charade.

A frog made jokes from a lily pad throne,
While a lizard spat rhymes in a tone.
"What do you call a fish with no eyes?"
Echoed the frog, as he sat all alone!

The leaves whispered secrets, giddy and bright,
Of squirrels who fancied themselves a sight.
"Have you seen Gus wearing that vest?"
The trees delighted in giggles at night.

With fireflies twinkling as a light show,
The critters gathered, feeling the glow.
In this laughter-soaked rendezvous,
Even the stars joined in on the flow!

Nature's Lingering Lyricism

In the thickets where oddities bloom,
A fox in a bow tie danced to a tune.
"Why did the chicken cross the park?"
It quipped as it twirled beneath the moon.

The flowers chuckled, petals aglow,
"Let's start a band!" cried a shy little crow.
With daisies on drums and sunflowers singing,
Harmony burst forth in a show!

Beetles boogied under the stars,
With each wiggle and giggle, they raised the bar.
"Dance like nobody's watching!" they cheered,
As blossoms lit up like small, twinkling jars.

Echoes of joy through the woods did spread,
As laughter and music blossomed instead.
Nature invited all to her ball,
Where humor and harmony danced ahead!

Untamed Phrases

In a garden where puns grow wild,
A humor-filled tale by a giggling child.
Words twist and turn in a playful chase,
Laughter erupts, we lose all grace.

A parrot squawks out a riddle,
As bees buzz by, feeling so little.
Tickled by whispers that twist in the air,
We tumble and crumble without a care.

Jokes bloom like daisies, bright and absurd,
While squirrels debate the sounds of a bird.
Each phrase a vine, creeping near,
And soon we're entangled, bursting with cheer.

So let the words dance, let them groove,
In this crazy jungle, we find our move.
With laughter our guide, let's wander and weave,
In this forest of phrases, we'll never leave.

Intricate Florals of Expression

Petals of laughter in colors so bold,
Whimsical whirls of stories retold.
A daffodil giggles at the plight of the rose,
While vines chuckle softly, nobody knows.

Tulips are gossipers, painting the scene,
Unruly and silly, oh what a keen!
The daisies dance with a wink and a grin,
While sunflowers bask in the comic din.

Swaying to rhythms of playful delight,
A patchwork of humor, oh what a sight!
As laughter unfurls in this floral disguise,
We find all the joy that's hidden in sighs.

Among blooms of nonsense, we wander and play,
With each flowing whim, we banter away.
In this garden of giggles, let's twirl and rewind,
For words like these are the best of their kind.

Echoes Beneath the Canopy

Beneath the green whispers of mischievous trees,
Lies a world of chuckles caught in the breeze.
Branches reach out for a wordplay embrace,
As shadows and sunshine dance in their space.

A squirrel takes notes in the leaves of the oaks,
While vines twist around, sharing their jokes.
The wind carries giggles, a sound so divine,
As thoughts spiral out like a playful design.

In the hush of the woods, where nonsense takes flight,
We gather the echoes of humor and light.
Each bark adds a punchline to nature's grand scene,
As laughter erupts, we're a wild, happy team.

So come join this folly, under canopy wide,
With vines interlaced, we'll flourish with pride.
In this orchard of quips, we'll savor the fun,
Where giggles and whispers meld into one.

Emotions Like Grapevines

Tangled emotions in rows so divine,
Each twist, each turn, like a glass of fine wine.
A joyride of feelings, so silly and sweet,
As we stumble through laughter, oh what a treat!

Ripe with amusement, we gather the fun,
A cluster of chuckles beneath the warm sun.
Each grape a reflection of jests we entwine,
As we sip on the magic from this playful vine.

A cork pops with giggles, the fizz fills the air,
As quirky emotions dance without care.
From blushes to banter, tangled in rhyme,
We savor each moment, transcending through time.

So raise up your glasses, let's toast with delight,
To emotions that flourish beneath joyful light.
In this vineyard of laughter, where humor aligns,
We'll drink deep of the joy that each moment defines.

www.ingramcontent.com/pod-product-compliance
Lightning Source LLC
Chambersburg PA
CBHW070313120526
44590CB00017B/2654